DINOSAURS, BEWARE!

✚ A Safety Guide ✚

Marc Brown and Stephen Krensky

LITTLE, BROWN AND COMPANY
New York ⌁ Boston

For endangered species everywhere

Library of Congress Cataloging in Publication Data

Brown, Marc Tolon.
  Dinosaurs, beware!

  Summary: Approximately sixty safety tips are demonstrated by dinosaurs in situations at home, during meals, camping, in the car, and in other familiar places.
  1. Children's accidents — Prevention — Juvenile literature. [1. Safety] I. Krensky, Stephen.
II. Title.
HV675.5.B76   363.1'075   82—15207
ISBN 0-316-11219-4 (pbk)   AACR2

PB: 20   19   18

SC

MANUFACTURED IN CHINA

Contents

At Home   4

In the Yard   8

During Meals   10

In Case of Fire   12

With Animals   14

On Wheels   16

At the Playground   18

When Camping   20

In the Car   21

At the Beach   22

On Short Trips   24

Giving First Aid   26

In Cold Weather   28

At Night   30

At Home

Don't play with matches.

Keep toys off the stairs.

Never play with electric sockets and plugs. They can shock you.

FOR BARNEY

HAPPY BIRTH BARNEY

4

A hot stove or heater can burn you. Don't touch either one.

Don't bang on glass doors or windo[ws]

Don't tell strangers who phone that you're home alone. Just say "Hello!" and ask them to leave a message.

Never play with the things stored under sinks or in medicine cabinets. They can make you very sick.

If an adult isn't home, don't let strangers into the house. Tell them to come back later.

7

In the Yard

Always put tools back where they belong.

Don't climb on thin branches.

8

During a thunderstorm, stay out of water and away from trees. Lightning often strikes in both places.

9

During Meals

Chew well before swallowing.

Don't lean back too far in your chair.

ay attention when using a sharp knife.

on't gulp hot foods. Taste them slowly.

11

In Case of Fire

Get outside as fast as possible, and don't stop to take along your favorite things.

If fire or heavy smoke is blocking y[our] door, shout for help out the windo[w]

smoke is making you cough, crawl along the floor. The air down there ill be easier to breathe.

Have a planned meeting place outside or your family. You'll know quickly f anyone is missing.

13

With Animals

Be very careful around a moth
animal and her young. She ma
think you want to hurt them.

Some animals will not be friendly.

Watch out!

ever move an injured animal by yourself.

Don't feed strange animals.

15

On Wheels

Use reflectors and lights for riding at night.

Don't show off.

Warn others of your approach with a bell or horn.

Obey all signs and traffic lights, and cross only at corners or crosswalks.

At the Playground

Stay alert while helping your friends learn new tricks.

Look before you leap.

Don't get on or off playground equipment suddenly.

When Camping

Learn which plants are poisonous to touch, and never taste strange berries, nuts, or mushrooms.

Stay on marked trails.

TO TAR PITS

Put out smoldering embers. They might start a new fire.

the Car

ways wear seat belts. If the car stops
ort, you won't keep going.

Don't play games with the driver.

eep your head and arms inside the windows.

21

At the Beach

Protect yourself from sunburn.

Wear a life jacket on a boat. It will keep you afloat if the boat doesn't.

Swim in pairs, and don't swim out over your head. A friend can warn you of danger.

22

Never overload a boat or raft.

On Short Trips

Always let someone know where you're going.

If you get lost, ask a police officer directions.

Walk on the sidewalk, not in the street.

24

Don't take rides from strangers.

arry your address, phone number, and some money in a safe place.

25

Giving First Aid

Clean a dirty scrape with soap and water before covering it with a bandage.

Put ice on a small burn to make it f better and heal faster.

Pull out splinters with tweezers.

Call an adult in case of serious inju

over a bee sting with mud or ice to soothe the itching and keep down the swelling.

In Cold Weather

Dress warmly, and go inside as soon as you get cold.

Never skate or walk on thin ice.

NO SKATING

Don't make tunnels under the snow. They could fall in on you.

ake sure the coast is clear.

29

At Night

If you hear strange noises, call an adult to investigate.

Never assume you know where everything is. Turn on a light.

Wear light-colored clothing when you go outdoors so you can be seen eas

ways use a flashlight.

So, dinosaurs, beware! Wouldn't you rather be safe than sorry?